Best New Poets in Canada
2018

BEST NEW POETS in CANADA 2018

Edited by
Kate Marshall Flaherty and Dane Swan

QUATTRO BOOKS

The publication of *Best New Poets in Canada 2018* has been generously supported by the Canada Council for the Arts and the Ontario Arts Council.

Cover design and typography: McNeill Design Arts
Editors: Kate Marshall Flaherty and Dane Swan

Library and Archives Canada Cataloguing in Publication

Best new poets in Canada, 2018 / Tara Borin, Sarah Kabamba, Georgia Wilder.

Poems.
Contents: Thick / by Tara Borin -- Maji / by Sarah Kabamba -- Atom-bomb nostalgia / by Georgia Wilder.
ISBN 978-1-988254-59-3 (softcover)

1. Canadian poetry (English)--21st century. I. Borin, Tara. Thick. II. Kabamba, Sarah. Maji. III. Wilder, Georgia, 1963- . Atom-bomb nostalgia.

PS8293.1.B49 2018   C811'.608   C2018-906433-1

Published by Quattro Books Inc.
Toronto
www.quattrobooks.ca

Printed in Canada

Contents

THICK
by Tara Borin

Maji
by Sarah Kabamba

Atom-Bomb Nostalgia
by Georgia Wilder

Preface

What a joy and challenge it was to read the nearly fifty manuscripts we received at Quattro for this inaugural contest and anthology. The ten on our shortlist were strong and varied, but the three poets who emerged as the finalists had particularly powerful and distinctive voices that we think represent new poets in Canada well. This trio of exciting collections fully embodies the lively diversity that characterizes our nation's culture at its leading edge.

Tara Borin's "Thick" is spare and striking. It explores the rough, beautiful and surprising inner and outer landscapes of a young poet mothering in the bush. The relationships of speaker to wild creatures and the beast that is child and parent are revealed through simple encounters and sharp images that resonate. The CanLit canon is filled with romanticized and glorified soliloquies on nature. Living in the wild isn't so glamorous. These poems bring the reader into the thick of the forest, the struggles and celebrations of rearing children in the isolated North, and the heaviness of pregnancy and parenthood, where "All you can do/is hope/you've whispered/the right incantations,/spilled enough blood/to appease –"

Sarah Kabamba's "Maji" is indeed like water, the way her writing flows from country to country, mother to daughter, mother tongue to new language, and from poetic form to poetic form exploring the hurdles a family faces emigrating from their physical and spiritual motherland. Love is thick as blood, as sea, as word and bond and memory. These poems get into your bones, and leave you tussled, thirsty, longing and paradoxically satisfied. The Swahili sprinkled into story adds spice, as do the poet's honesty, home truths, recipes and searching reflections. Reading these poems is a journey deep into the complex and compassionate personhood and life of the speaker, who invites self and reader to "try to build rooms in bodies/ you will learn that some people leave anyways,/abandon the homes you built, break down/the walls, leave empty rooms/you will learn that you will/love anyways."

Georgia Wilder's "Atom Bomb Nostalgia" ticks with a mix of nostalgia and new paradigms; her command of language and form makes for daring and drama that challenges the reader while giving delight. Here are poems that cut deep, that have weight to them, intensity, and a fearlessness that creates a path few poets dare to tread. The love poems are charged and electric, the criticisms scathing, the allusions alluring, and the scope of information and historical detail broad and boldly woven in. Wilder's poems jump off the pages – in protest, in pleading, in pleasures – and announce their presence with a prophetic voice: "I am the hope of displaced/millions. More will come./For all those who know this road from Damascus/may scales now fall from your eyes."

Kate Marshall Flaherty and Dane Swan

THICK
by
Tara Borin

These poems are for Jamie and Anna,
who watched my kids while I was putting this manuscript together;
and for my parents, who always believed I could do it.

Planet Motherhood

Primordial violence
delivers me
into a wilderness unfamiliar.

Those who've come before are twigs
snapped underfoot –
I never see them.

They stake their claim with
bits of flagging tape,
neon prayer flags
tied to trees.

I read the map
scribbled on my skin,
follow grasses bent
by others

but remain lost.

My children, restless,
trail me with tantrums
thrown in zero gravity,
rebounding for days.

Moon-father orbits, elliptical.
We try to draw him down –
oh, how we howl.

Each morning I strain
to touch my feet to soil,
to catch
my breath

but
I never do.

Hawk

For days,
a hawk haunts our clearing.

We watch it take down
        a fat brown squirrel,

my boys in a hush
on the porch.

The hawk
rips another strip.

My baby cries
for milk:
hawk, startled,
takes flight.

Carcass abandoned,
black spill of blood on grass:
the kids rush to look.

I perch
on the porch step,
breast bared,
my contented baby sighs.

Hawk circles,
screams.

Advice for New Mothers

Dress them in darkness,
your prayers star-stitched
into their skin

fill their pockets
with salt

bestow your kisses
like coins
on their eyelids

let them slip
into a forest of swaying bodies –
cords still pulsing.

All you can do
is hope
you've whispered
the right incantations,
spilled enough blood
to appease –

Nuisance

Only the thickness of log
and triple-paned glass
between my children and
the open maw
of a bear.

I slip warm chocolate chip
cookies from the pan
to the cooling rack –
their father loads the gun.

He fires a warning shot
from the porch
while the kids lick
the mixing bowl,
unbothered
as the bear.

The conservation officer
brings a culvert trap
baited with
bacon, canned pineapple.

We could put out
a plate of cookies,
like for Santa,
the kids say.

Later, bedtime routine
interrupted
by a metallic bang –
the trap slams shut.

The bear
peers toward the house,
sees the real nuisance.

Conservation officer returns,
we watch from the window
as they hitch trap to truck.
They'll haul it across
two rivers, mountains,
hundreds of kilometers
from our poorly-secured garbage,
our fresh-baked cookies.

Relocated, dozing
in a distant meadow,
the bear dreams
of my children
running through
his forest, eating
his berries,
their faces
swimming under glass
like salmon in
churning water.

Spark

My little acolytes
gather 'round me.

We kneel
before the cold woodstove,

autumn morning textured
in damp grey flannel.

They hand me balls
of crumpled up *Yukon News*,

watch me make a nest
inside a log cabin

of birch kindling
I split in the yard.

Daughter passes me the box of Redbirds.
I slide out a match, drag it

along the sandpapered strip.
It sizzles alight –

scents of sulfur tickle my nose,
conjure memory –

a girl's darkened bedroom,
glow of streetlight through the window:

she sits cross-legged
on the dusty rose carpet,

lights candles, whispers spells,
peers into the future, but

can't see us
peering back.

I am a flower
blooming in reverse:

petals close in on themselves,
bud-tight,
tuck back into earth
seed-bound,

waiting to be released
by fire.

Bush kids

teethe on rocks;

suckle sweet water as it springs
from Earth's hummock teat;

comb wild raspberries, rain wet,
into their mouths, not noticing
tiny green worms secreted within;

fall asleep to
the woodstove's lullaby tick,
the thrum of mating grouse in spring and

in dreams,
chase Orion's dogs
through black spruce forests.

Homestead

Out here it doesn't matter
if I never get dressed,
chop wood in my long underwear,
squat lazily outside the cabin
under canted spruce.

There's no one around
to hear me yell
at the kids,
or see me spank
the oldest
when he bites
the baby.

Weeds don't matter;
petunias dying in their pots
don't matter,
because only the whiskey jack
ever stops for tea.

I can't refuse, so
invite her in,
ask about her soot-coloured young:
have they fledged, can they fend
for themselves.

She tilts her head, claws
on the lip of my mug,
her black-bright eyes critical
of my featherless children, so

I shoo her off,
cast her out
with the cold
dregs
of my tea.

Visitor

Yardful of dozing dogs
suddenly alert –
they strain and bark
like someone's here:
I look out to see

a wolf –

gasp –
at the edge of the clearing,
its head a dark wedge
splitting heavy hoarfrost shiver
like birch logs split
in snapping cold.

I've heard they send out a young one
to befriend the dogs,
playful for a few days until
trust is born then it
lures them into the bush
for the ravenous pack.

Let them lure me out
instead.

I'll stoke the fire,
tuck the puling baby
into the wood-box
his perfect stove-length
with waiting logs;
leave breakfast dishes
unwashed in the sink,

the dogs chained
in the yard –

Self-care

Our cabin is nap-quiet; the silence smokes like a starter pistol. I pick my way through the fling of toys, slip on my bunny boots and work gloves and hurry out to gather an armload of wood. Inside, I rouse the fire. At the washstand I fill a chipped white enamel basin with hot water from the kettle on the woodstove, peel off wool sweater, army surplus thermal undershirt, old Tragically Hip t-shirt, wool socks, long underwear salted with dead skin. I hang my head over the basin: dip cup into clear water and pour. Dip and pour. Water soaks my thick hair. Squeeze shampoo into palm, scrub my itchy scalp. Water drips down my forehead, over my shoulders and back, warm fingers touching me where no one else does. I wrap my wet hair in a towel, carry the basin over to the couch in front of the fire. I put on a fresh pair of long underwear, pulled up at the ankles, ease my feet into the water, clouded now with spent soap suds. The warm water prickles my feet, phantom limbs remembered. I lean back into the cushions, watching the flames consume the wood as the light of the brief day fades from the flickering room. I hold my breath, listening, on borrowed time.

Portrait of a SAHM

teetering
on the edge

of her couch,
an asteroid belt
of dirty laundry,
books, LEGO
and children
hurtling, relentless.

Like mice, little hands
run up
and down the clock,
pat-a-cake pendulum breasts,
broken hourglass hips –
sand's run out but

they keep turning her over,
a pebble worn smooth
by fingers reaching
in a pocket close and dark.

Quietly, she implodes –
a scatter of sand sifting
through chubby fingers,
and still
they keep
turning
and
turning
her
over.

Wild Strawberries

Like one of the dogs,
ears cocked for the crunch
of tires
in the gravel drive,
your footfalls
on the porch steps,

I drop the kids
and run,
chase mountains to
pavement's end.

Wild strawberries
throw their scarlet creepers
onto the dirt shoulder:
they reach for me, snag
my feet and drag me
into the ditch,
coil tight,
hold me.

Birds, bears
browse
in the lazy heat.

Trembling aspen offer up
their soft applause.

I watch the fruits,
        no bigger than the tip
        of my baby's pinky
ripen
just out of tongue's reach.

My children come,
pick the patch clean:
their berry-stained fingers
brush over my concealment.

Silent,
I remain caught
in a wild embrace.

Applause fades.
Gilded leaves
bury me further, then
snow edges
down from the mountains –
deep freeze
settles in.

Next spring, my bones
will blossom with saw-toothed
strawberry leaves,
what's left of me
will dribble
in a burst of sweetness
down the chins
of my children.

Balm

In a cove of willow
with the girl from St. Eustache –
    who barely spoke a lick
    of English –
her fluent fingers translated
my body's tongue,
the river shushing by.

Would she be surprised
to see me now,
stuck in some forgotten slough,
children mired about my legs,
chanting:
your body's not your own –

would she lead me once more
into those willows far away,
the river susurrant:
ça va aller, ça va aller.

Rise

I peer out from between my ribs
at a sunrise that spreads
like blood spat on a scrim
of snow,

heart heavy-breathing
in my left ear

while around me
little beasts monster
under backlit trees,

startle smaller birds so that
eggs fall from nests,
crushed
beneath careless feet,

rip flower heads
from stems
with cutting teeth.

      I'd rather hide
      inside this body cavity,
      surf systole waves
      back to sleep.

But day begins
when the sky turns ordinary,
when the beasts howl:

they need me

      to kiss finger tips
      to peel an orange –
      their hold can crack ribs.

Afterstorm

We walk through woods,
the forest floor

more forgiving
after the storm,

leaves of lungwort and wild rose
shimmering, rain-jewelled.

The kids race ahead,
free of the house;

like the dog,
they don't come when I call.

Bright jackets flashing,
they lope through dense

lichen-draped spruce
until I can't see them anymore.

As with the dog,
I try to trust

they'll find their way home,
hair wet and clinging

to their foreheads,
try to trust that

they'll wait for me
there.

Birdwatching

I once watched birds.
Spent hours alone
on the rocky river bank,
in the willows,
on a cliff's edge.

Watched a bald eagle
defend its catch
against gulls,
a common merganser
teach her ducklings to dive.

I could distinguish
three different warblers
by song alone,
never went anywhere
without my binoculars.

Now, three kids deep,
my binoculars
gather dust
and sightings
are incidental –

a boreal owl soars over
the driveway
where we kick a ball.
A sharp-tailed grouse, rare,
dances in our yard.

In the car on the way to the playgroup
we pass a float of ducks
on an unruffled pond;
I long to name them,
feel frantic that I can't.

I've forgotten the warblers, but
have learned
to tell the difference
between a tired cry
and a hungry one,

have learned that
neither birds
nor children
belong to me.

No Signal

Our
connec-
tion
is
brok-
en.

They expect
me
to fix
every
thing.

To begin,
put the
useless
phone
down.

Next,
plug
bundled
baby
onto hip,
tag two brothers
behind:
an ellipsis
trailing
the property line.

Then,
check
for tracks
left
in fresh snow:

lynx's paws
flower
across hare's twin
exclamations;
a message
that needs
no
receipt.

Let the children
trample
the hushed marks
of animals,
write a new story
in snow where
their smaller
impressions
disappear
inside my
larger ones.

In the gathering dark,
we find
each other –
lights
blinking on
one
by
one.

Shed Things

I ate their placentas
cooked with garlic,
ginger and lemongrass,
the leftovers forgotten
in the back of the freezer.

Cord stump shock
dried and fallen away –
the hard black nub
shifted around my dresser
until one day,
brushed to the floor.
I swept it up
with other shed things.

I kept their baby teeth,
fairy taken,
in my jewelry box:
they chatter
each time I look
for my good earrings.

First curls I clipped
at the picnic table in the yard:
the wind took them,
the birds plucked them
for their nests –

my mother,
memory-keeper,
wept.

Spring

Some days I am a black billow
of clouds that choke
their horizon.

I trudge through the thick,
oblivious to miracles
both large and
small:

frost's retreat,
sun-touched,

last summer's shoes,
outgrown,

a wood frog's heart,
reanimated.

A startle of grouse or
a child's hand
slipped into mine
causes me to
bud –

bursting,
the world
greens like a smile.

Acknowledgements

I am grateful to the following literary magazines for publishing earlier versions of these poems:

"Visitor," "Homestead" in *Mused Bella Online Literary Magazine*, March 2016

"Balm" (Formerly "The Girl from St. Eustache") in *Rat's Ass Review* Love and Ensuing Madness Series, March 2016

"Rise" in *Uppagus*: Issue 19, August 2016

"Wild Strawberries" in *Yellow Chair Review*, September 2016

"Portrait of a Stay at Home Mom" (formerly "Touched Out") in *Uppagus*: Issue 20, October 2016

"Spring" in *Mom Egg Review* Vol. 15, April 2017

"Birdwatching" in *The Maynard*, October 2017

"Hawk," "Bush Kids" in *The Northern Review*, November 2017

The term "snapping cold" used in "Visitor" comes from Tr'ondëk Hwëch'in elder JJ Van Bibber, as recounted in his book *I Was Born Under a Spruce Tree* (Friesens, 2012).

I am so thankful to live and write as an uninvited guest on the traditional territory of the Tr'ondëk Hwëch'in.

Kate Marshall Flaherty, thank you for helping to polish these poems with your keen eye, and for all your encouragement. To the judges at Quattro Books, thank you for giving me a chance.

Maji

by
Sarah Kabamba

For my parents, Robert and Arlette Kabamba, always

Cycles

water is about history, history is about ripples, ripples repeat, create waves, waves make seas make oceans make tsunamis make floods. water leaks from ribcages, there are people who hold oceans inside of them, turn them inside out and press them to your ear, hear their stories like the lullaby of the sea in a shell, shells are about echoes, echoes are about listening and listening is about remembering is about forgetting but the sea never forgets – remember time does not always heal, sometimes it rips you open, reopens wounds until you're bleeding nostalgia and your blood is a story because veins are about roads are about roots, are about connections, are about family ties older than rivers, than oceans, than seas and tides dance to the moon's song, long to leap into the sky, to become air, stars, constellations, galaxies, worlds. the wolves in my heart are howling, sending messages to the sky, the stars, and the man on the moon is crying for the sun. someone should tell them *shhhh* there is beauty in darkness.

Regeneration

some mornings i wake
my body so heavy with memories
i break trying to hold them in –
words bleed from the darkness
of my mouth; the crack of my ribs
gives birth to my heart
over & over again

my body doesn't recognize itself,
wants to smash all mirrors
i see my mother in the back
of my eyes, my grandmother
in the ridges of my palms

i am heavy with every woman
before me –
my blood cries
lost from its source

Some days

the weight of bones
makes my skin ache,
the history in my blood
becomes too heavy
i want to shed
dead skin memories
words sit uneasy in the back of my throat
they gather multiply stumble over one another –
some days i swallow more than i say
bite my tongue 'til my mouth is full
with blood oceans
i swim lost in my mother's
tongue, swahili waves in salt water skin,
dead language in my bloody teeth

No one tells you

there'll be times when your bones
                feel like they are floating in your skin,
your body will be so bloated with home-
                sickness that you will want
to slice yourself open
                clean-cut to the ribs
quick, like gutting a fish
                you will search for home in people,
try to build rooms in bodies
                you will learn that some people leave anyways,
abandon the homes you built, break down
                the walls, leave empty rooms
you will learn that you will
                love anyways

sunshine & sadness

you have carried this melancholy in your skin for so long
it's like your body doesn't know how to be without sadness

the women in your family deal in grief
which is to say they're familiar with loss

accustomed to building homes out of absences
mama tells you the women in your family deal in survival

which is to say your very existence is magic.

Exodus

here is how it begins –
with children.

tell me, do you know
what a mother would do
for love, for the water she
carried in her womb, for delivery

is bitter
sweet pain and joy
life and death and
prophet and loss
hold on and let

go. release

is sweet
bitter becoming
and unbecoming, ravelling and
unravelling, hand-woven womb
shifts, water breaks, blood
gushes.

Jochebed is sinking.

tell me, can you carry this child?
is this what she cried to the Nile,
what Mariam sang as she followed
the rush of water to

royalty. royal feet do not touch the ground,
do not feel the heat of desert, sand,
dust, the never-ending grit, their castles
floating on water. a baby is
pulled from the sea. he does not belong

to you.

tell me, would you put your child
on a sinking ship
if there is no better option
than drowning?

Roads

i.
mama is always watching and
reading on the news back home,
she says to me: people are dying,
they are killing people, we are
waters and waves away, but there
are ripples in my skin, that i
can't really explain, and you

ask me why
i don't write love poems,
i know you're really asking
why don't you write about me?

but when it comes down to it
isn't everything a love poem?
don't blame me because you
can't recognize it, you say
tell me what you're afraid of

i say roads

i know you don't understand
when your roads have always
been paved, you take for granted
the bodies beneath them

ii.
papa needs a visa to enter his home
country, the officers at the border
pass our passports around
we wait and wait, i fall asleep
on my suitcase, i've been dreaming
of drowning for days

i wake up with a mouth
full of salt, my body aches
like an open wound, they pull
us into a dusty office, the president's
picture hangs on the wall, they tell us
we have to give them money to cross

the taxi rumbles over dirt roads
red sand flies in the air, the car keeps
stopping, the driver doesn't seem
surprised as he opens the hood
to twine two wires together,
a spark in the dust, the hiccup
of the engine, and we're off again

but then there are official and
makeshift checkpoints, men with
guns, and there is money, money
must always switch hands, and
when the car sputters to a stop
in front of one of the presidential
buildings, the driver whispers to us
that people have gotten shot for
stopping here

iii.
we continue
rattling over dirt roads
i stare out the window
papa tells stories about the spots
we pass, i try and memorize
places, names, the sound
of his voice, i hold my heart
breath in my hands
this beating, this blood,
tombstones in my ribs
my motherland
is breaking
me

Table

here is how it begins –
with wood. maybe my ancestors built
villages, boats, statues

here is what i know to be true:

there is a tree in the backyard
of my father's childhood home
that my grandfather planted
for my grandmother

now that house belongs to a political party
we asked the soldiers' permission to enter
so my father could show me
the tree is still there

inside, walls have been knocked down;
my father shows me where his room
would have been, the kitchen, the living room,

he says, *there wasn't a lot of furniture*
but there was a small wooden table
here, we would gather around it
your grandfather, grandmother, uncles, aunts
one of your uncles took it with him

this is how it continues –
with wood. maybe i will plant
a forest, build a raft, a bridge.

here is what i know to be true:

the wood of the kitchen table is scarred;
there are marks where my sister
carved her name, marker doodles
run up the wooden legs, it wasn't always
this table, there was another one

different wood, a different room,
a different house, a different continent
but some things are the same:
discussions, debates, a young child
finds her voice, there are disagreements
but there is also love, there is always love

there is laughter, warm cups of tea
and beignets, sticky brown hands,
talks of the future, the present, the past,
ancestors – the original freedom fighters,
revolutionaries, contradictions of history

my father tells me that his mother was
the strongest woman he knows,
how she once yelled at the wife
of my grandfather's boss
for disrespecting my grandfather.
she told my father
don't name your daughters after me
why?
because women suffer too much

i wonder what would she have thought
of me

am i

what my ancestors dreamed of,
because they've given me more
than i could dream of,
i don't need to beg for a seat at a table
where there's no room for their spirits.

Things i am learning:

i.

the importance of language

mama i am sorry, i forgot my first love, my first tongue, the sounds that i was born with. i can't speak to my aunty. it makes me want to weep, cry myself back into my mother's womb. my tears don't know what country they're in. my sorrow nomadic. but i'm done chasing her. i'm letting her go. teach me rebirth. let me relearn.

ii.

the importance of naming

my brothers are named after my grandparents. my aunty cries when we go see her. my god. my god. she repeats my father's father's names. my father's mother's names. tells me, look, my parents are not dead; they have come back to me.

iii.

the importance of history

my roots are thick, tangled. i am just beginning to unravel them. discovering there is no beginning. no end. just a continuation. this family tree is ancient. but still, it has just begun to bloom.

iv.

the importance of being present

i've been walking more, letting red dust stain my skin. speaking to relatives. listening to stories. collecting poetry. realizing not all moments must be documented. it's enough to be; i am enough. i am here.

v.

the importance of stories

i've been listening. unapologetic in my quietness. my father starts many sentences with *let me tell you a story*. i spend mornings listening to my uncle speak of my grandparents, of past lives, of borders. of crossings. of naming. here, i have felt an outpouring. a bleeding of art. i am in no rush to stanch it.

vi.
the importance of parents

everyone says i look like my mother. her childhood friend touches my face.
asks me, *how is it that your mother gave birth to herself?* my father shows me
the roads where she used to gather charcoal, the market where she used to
sell beignets, my brother tied to her back. i inherited my father's quietness,
his love for words. they tell me he always had a book with him. he's telling his
own story now, a slow documentation that i am so thankful for. when i was
younger i was worried about becoming my parents. now i am scared i won't.

vii.
the importance of recognizing where you come from

mama told me. don't fall in love with a man who is in love with his
motherland. then what is there to say of me? half girl. half woman. in love
with a land i still don't really know. i've been walking where my parents
walked, seeing where they stayed. my god, they have come from far. the act of
remembering isn't always pretty. you can't change memory. i wouldn't want
to. because of it i am who i am.

viii.
homesickness is real

i do not yet know its importance. only that it is real. my first day back home
uncle says i am *dépaysé.* i throw up my dinner, barely speak to anyone. i feel
a fatigue that makes my bones ache. i cry myself to sleep in a strange bed. i
miss home. but i do not know which home i am crying for.

Stream

i step, bleary-eyed
curly-haired onto
cold bathroom tile,
i think to myself, i am
not brave, i can't step
into the shower
without testing the water
first. in her hometown, mama
used to walk miles every morning
to get water. i think how, even here
she makes us boil water before
we drink it. i recall random
facts, like the boiling point of
water is 100°C. some deserts used
to be oceans. we breathe water
before we breathe air. i'm not
saying i understand what
it all means (see there's still so
much i don't know), like the
proper ratio of pasta to
water, how to cook small amounts
and some days i don't eat because
my body is bloated with nostalgia
but i know to cut the heat
when the water starts to
bubble or else it'll boil over.
i know how to say drowning
in three different languages
noyade
zama majini
drowning

i'm losing one of them
and i never learned how
to swim.

sometimes i hear
oceans calling my names,
i wonder if mama wonders
how she got this wanderer
who's always late because
she's composing sonnets in
the shower; i wonder if she
ever feels like a mermaid
out of water – split tail, split tongue
split in half – see,
she splits sea
shells by the seashore
searching
for the sea
mama, is your tongue in knots?
because there's a whirlpool in my mouth,
there's the home you lost, the sisters
you were supposed to have, the family
you left behind, there's me swallowing
myself and you
knocking on the bathroom
door, saying:
turn off the shower already,
you're using too much water.

Questions for Mama

mama, for as long as i've known you, you've always been a quiet woman, never really talked a lot. when i was younger, you would braid my hair into thick plaits, singing as you drew the strands in, out, over, under, like silk in your calloused hands. i'd sit between your legs and trace the veins in your feet. i liked to think of where your feet had been before me, before they crossed a continent, broke skies, scattered seas.

your voice would echo in the shells of my ear; while i sat at your feet trying not to cry – my roots tangled, and my hair nappy. you'd always tell me *there's no beauty without pain* and i always wanted to ask, mama, how did you come to know the beauty of pain so well?

you carry yourself like a night without stars – beautiful, deep, silent. where did you learn to be powerfully still, to make silences speak? how did you manage to bear the weight of absence so well, for so long? because, mama, after seeing you lose your two sisters, i know grief sits heavy in the back of your throat. you learned to take sadness and turn it into strength. i see it in the arch of your spine, felt it running through your fingers, as you braided my hair, drew those strands in, out, over, under. mama, even after being in school for so many years, i realize that those moments at your feet taught me more than any degrees.

that's why, no matter where i may wander, i will always return to your skies; i will always come back to your shores. water always returns to its source and i will always find myself in you.

Home Recipes

moja.
you find yourself
in the "ethnic" aisle of supermarkets;
fill your cart with
plantains yams cassava
okra nutmeg cinnamon

mbili.
it hurts to think
you broke the sky to get here –
when the plane took off, your heart
fell through your body, straight
through your calloused feet;
your husband laughed,
said it was just the turbulence

tatu.
the oven and all four stove
burners are fired up,
the kitchen smells like
your mother's home;
sweet stickiness of ripe plantain
nutmeg and cinnamon cling to
your dark skin like a memory

nne.
you buy stacks of phone cards;
the Senegalese man who owns
the corner store calls you sister,
tells you the best brands for calling home
but they all look the same to you –
brightly colored yellows, reds, oranges
or picturesque sunsets with baobab trees,
giraffes, tigers, lions, and elephants

tano.
it's dusk outside now,
night hugs the edges of sky,
creeps under your door
into the hot kitchen where you cook
and cook, until you can't tell if it's sweat
or tears on your face;
your food is always too salty
and stings the open wounds
in your mouth left by broken words
and lost language

sita.
you feel like you are pushing out a continent
when your first daughter is born;
when she learns to speak, people say
you're lucky she won't have an accent at all –
english rests heavy in your mouth, words full of
jagged edges and sharp blades;
home coats your words like blood –
your accent reminds english
that here, in your body, it is not the native

saba.
when your husband comes home
broken body   broken bones
he smells the spices in your skin
as you exchange whispers with
broken tongues   broken languages
you find home in your tired bodies
nutmeg underneath your dirty fingernails
and paprika in your braids

nane.
if there's a recipe for home
you haven't found it yet

Palate

salt.
she's not scared of people leaving.
what terrifies her is what remains in
the stench of their absences, the holes
she has to keep filling to hide these phantom bodies.
she cuts onions without crying; her mother
always told her the trick was to press her tongue
into the roof of her mouth. she presses down
on the knife, cuts into her palm.
sometimes when he kisses her, she bites down
on his lip so she can taste the sea.
she massages spices into red meat
the same way she touches him – wet hands,
salt clinging to skin.

sour.
the day after their wedding night, she washes
the sheets with vinegar and water.
he whistles as he goes out to the fields. she braids
yellow beads into her hair, rubs lemon juice
into her skin. the goat's milk always comes out sour.
he drinks it anyways, wipes his mouth with
the back of his hand; his knuckles are always bruised.
he brings her bleeding sunsets. she sits at the kitchen table
and picks thorns out of her palms.

bitter(sweet).
because they are one and the same,
he comes home from the fields,
grass and mud clinging to his skin.
she picks straw from his hair and makes dolls,
washes the earth out of his clothes. dirt clings
to her skin, crawls underneath her fingernails, smudges
on backbone ridges when she touches him. when he yawns,
the cloying smell of roses fills the room.
the walls smell different when he's home.
she opens up all the windows in the house
when he's gone, scrubs at the bedsheets
until her arms are sore.

umami.
because sometimes nothing
in english can say it, she ties her tongue
in knots, slips swahili syllables into the cracks
of voices, words, spaces, skin.
he begins to forget, tells her she must
learn english, speaks over her at grocery stores,
restaurants, parties, the kitchen table.
she sings lullabies in lost languages, her voice
bouncing off the walls long after he is gone. it fills
the spaces he's left behind. she pulls herself out
of his absences, teaches her daughter
how to cut onions without crying.

How To Forget a Language:

i.

take all the ice trays in your empty house,
chew ice 'til your gums bleed and your mouth freezes,
'til your tongue forgets the taste of language,
'til you forget that in a village in Kinshasa
your grandmother sat under the shade of baobab trees,
fried peanuts and cassava with hands lined like ancient
trees and told stories in Swahili

ii.

write words on every inch of your body
then fill up the tub with water so hot
it steams up the bathroom and blisters your skin,
wait 'til the water darkens with unsaid words,
'til the memory of speech swells into oceans,
'til the water rejects your body and your limbs grow
too heavy for your skin, 'til you forget what it means
to run, even though your father's absence taught you
to be a nomad long before you could walk

iii.

open all the windows and doors
'til wind fills the house and finds you,
let its cold breath brace your skin 'til
you lose the stories in your goosebumps
and your veins forget their source

Dislocation

a forgotten tongue
the absence of speech
broke my jaw

the crack of bones,
realignment of ribs,
pain of dislocation
make it hard to breathe
and my breaths don't know
what language they're in

my tears have nowhere
to return to because I've erased
the shoreline and swallowed the sea –
i am drowning in my own mouth

my wet hands ache
for language, grasp for words –
pound, pull, mould, force them
back into my mouth 'til they fit,
'til they begin to feel familiar
but there's a war in my mouth

i can try to hide it but my lips crack,
'til my gums bleed, my teeth break, saliva
and blood pool under my bruised tongue –
see, the body remembers
what the mind cannot.

Split

my mother
land is breaking me
& he asks: *how can you still love
her?* he could never love anything so dreadful.
he tastes the saltiness of my skin,
says *there's something there
something here between us
is there
someone else?*

no (yes)
see, what i mean is
it's just that
every day i wake up
& swallow a continent, push
oceans to the back of my throat
while stories drenched in salt
  leak
  from my ribcage

stay / home

i.
stay

this land made him
a soldier before he was born
a prisoner of war in his mother's skin
his father an ache
his heart carries

& she reminds him
of home – split skin
& splintered bone
yes, it hurts
but he's never wanted
to stay before

ii.
home

he smells like home
but these days home smells
like war & smoke;
she's tired of burning & the ashes she carries
in her bones are heavy & all her body
knows is to run

some nights her body is a battleground,
landmines going off under his touch
he carries bombs beneath his tongue
& kisses her like it's his last breath

Dust

he traces the curve of my spine,
tells me he wants
to go back to Sierra Leone;
i want to ask him
how can he love a mother-
land that masticated him –
left him
a crushed carcass
not even vultures would touch.
when i open my mouth
all i can taste is grittiness
i'm scared
he'll smell the graveyard i carry
between my lips

Salt Trails

mama warned me about men
like dead seas, like drowning
didn't want to breathe
didn't want this
my body
lids dried up
i think i am becoming
waxing, waning,
do you feel
do you hear me
why don't you
why can't i

like you, men who smell like salt,
i fell into you
didn't want to want you
feeling, all of the water leaving
the back of my eye
salt trails on melanin
      the moon
full
my pull
calling out the wild in you
let go
let go

Touch

how easily skin scabs
bruises form continents
it surprises you how
much pain the body
can create   contain
        give birth to

your veins
have not yet bled out
the pains of labour do not compare
to the night she was conceived
the shuddering ghost pains that ran through
your body when you realized your daughter
looked like somebody else
and you wanted
to swallow her whole
so she'd belong
to you
only you

when she grabbed your finger
with her tiny dark fist
you realized how one can be
both hard and soft

Enough

the heat in your blood is enough to warm your body
sometimes flames feel like home, and the smell of burned
bodies and charred skin blocks your nose,
sits heavy in your skin, sometimes you remember
how he tried to put you out, how he pressed himself
into you until skin melted and gave birth to
bone

teaching your daughter to read water:

i.
first you must realize the sea
has seen more bodies than some cemeteries,
that ripples retain history and play it back
like an echo, that the water has stolen your
reflection and you will never get it back –
until you learn to become a drop, let
the waves sing to you, learn songs
that cradled bodies, broke chains
and lured captains to their graves,
remember oceans hold every shade of blue;
so must you.

ii.
remember to pass it on,
teach your daughters
how to read waves,
how to translate the oceans in their bones.
tell them
you can always swim back to yourself.

Carry

my parents are the best
kind of poetry, which is to say
they are profound without meaning to be,
intricate in their simplicity

my father, in the living room
surrounded by family,
eats fresh-cooked cassava and peanuts,
corn on the cob burnt with charcoal;
dark bottles of malt sweat on the table
he looks at my mother, laughs, says
we are a sacrificed generation
we did what we had to
so now our children don't have to
the women and men laugh, nod, saying, *ndiyo, ndiyo, ndiyo*

in the kitchen i drown
my hands in the sink;
the women bring their laughter
into the room, flood me
with brightly colored cloths, spices,
warm bodies, swahili
i close my eyes, this is how
i want to be carried away

the women pull pots and pans from shelves,
fill plates with sliced plantains and yams,
gut fish with bare hands – blood is too familiar
with their skin, yet they still sing, still dance, still
let their bodies sway, their voices
weaving in and out; oil sizzles, sauce bubbles,
scents mix, and spices colour the air
i open my eyes, this is how
i want to be carried away

they laugh at my quietness,
kitchen heat surrounds
us, makes my mother's cheeks glisten
as she tells the story of how i did not cry
for an hour after i was born; she holds so many
stories; some she tells often, some
we rarely speak of, she says to me
if you let it, grief will kill parts of you

knowing her story, all i can say is
mama, teach me the language of survival
she says, *sometimes it sounds too much like sadness,*
sister languages   let me teach you joy

my parents have given me poetry without knowing
i have been collecting their words, storing them
in my bones; i will never lose them

Acknowledgements

Much thanks to the editors of the following publications for publishing the following poems, some as earlier versions:

"Cycles," "Dust" appeared in *Room Magazine* 39.1: Women of Colour (2016)

"Regeneration" (as "Generations"), and "stay / home" (as "Stay" appeared in *In/Words Magazine & Press* Special Themed Issue: Refuge(e) (2016)

"Exodus" appeared in *Canthius* 05 (2018)

"Home Recipes" (as "Recipes for Home") and "How to Forget a Language:" (as "This is how you Forget a Language:") appeared in *The New Quarterly* Issue 143 (Summer 2017)

"Palate" and "Teaching Your Daughter to Read Water" appeared in *HA&L Magazine* 10.2: Storied Lives (2017-18)

"Carry" was shortlisted for the 2017 *CBC Poetry Prize*

"Roads" appeared in *In/Words Magazine and Press* Special Issue: Dis(s)ent (2018)

I would like to thank Quattro Books for giving me a chance to be part of such a beautiful collection. I am also grateful to Kate Marshall Falherty for her help, encouragement, and just generally being a great guide throughout this process. Thank you also to Dane Swan for his sharp eye to detail in the editing process. Lastly, thank you to anyone who may read this, you are greatly appreciated.

Atom-Bomb Nostalgia

by
Georgia Wilder

Part 1: Parting Ways

Invocation

I greet you at
the threshold
of myself in half
sleep, half-naked

light with love and joy
(both open wounds)

I am grateful
for your curses:
broken mirrors
raided graves
hormonal nights of
lunar heat and
stifled howls

you, muses
necromance
my fallen tree
recalling
supple joints

ghost-limbs still
felt within

you send me exiled
migrants: crowded
wooden boats of
weeping timber

needy strangers
(lost familiars
doppelganger'd)
seeking refuge

I try to flesh the voices
you assemble here
on this

my tidal strand.

Marielle
for Marielle Franco

In the favela *Maré,* Marielle gathers crowds
speaking against militias, drug-lords. She is single
mother, African, Brazilian, leader of the Lesbian
Front. She vows to find the source of bullets that ravage
the homes of the poor.

Rio at dusk, on the eve of Fat Tuesday, I watch
bearded men with gauzy wings farcically kissing in
macho streets. Mustachioed drunk girls titter
in bi-curious embrace: red devil revelers, irreverent nuns,
singing troupes of giant phalluses skip through the crowds
as if there were nothing to fear.

Half-divine, half-bird, exiled monarchs return
to the masquerade: drag queens and trans-folk
secretly reign, disguised as everyone else.

I walk in the theme parks of danger almost till dawn
from Ipanema through Copacabana beach past the
Sugar Loaf cable cars through the Arcos de Lapa
graffiti-tagged, colonial palace façades. The streets
pungent rivers, perfumed with piss and beer.

By daylight, the world is upside down. Olympic graft;
purchased politicians. Gunmen and Zika invade the favelas.
Both are gaining ground.

Marielle promises change.

The smoggy sky signals Ash Wednesday.
I travel: São Paulo, between airports
a route dotted with neon signs for sex shops.

In Rio, Marielle rallies women, sisters of the slums.
She raises voices in their mouths, feeds them
parts of herself as they fast in supplication.

Halfway to Easter resurrection, she tweets: the bullets
belong to police. She knows who her executioners are.

On a distant mountain, the unflinching statue
of Christ the Redeemer, arms outstretched, continues
as always to face the other way.

Skin

I am buried
deep under my skin
beneath layers of fat
and insomnia's din.

In the place where I'm buried
my true self is thin.

In the place where I'm missing
the fingers creep in and
finger the darkness
under my skin.

I am buried
awake but inside.
I am small as a cat
where a cat goes
to hide.

I am loose in my skin
where creatures abide.

I could drink in a corner
and let the day slide.
I could swallow the chatter
that scares me inside.

In verses I gather
the folds of my skin.
I breathe in a sea
where the voices begin.

I break through a surface
transparent and thin
to harrow the words
from under my skin.

For John, When We Danced to Purple Rain

Funny how summer rain reminds me of dancing,
reminds me of nearly forgotten lovers.

'Funny', we said, not 'tragic' or 'ironic'. We
laughed rejecting labels so predictably defined. We

laughed watching Elmer Fudd sing cartoon words
to the Flight of the Valkyries. We

laughed reading Sontag, who said Wagner
could never be camp. I met you in a ménage à trois:

soft as a woman you laughed, knowing there
was nothing we could fake. We joked at

the glitter that wouldn't come off.
We laughed at our ridiculous nakedness,
at our muscular common denominator:

a short Rock Hudson in crotch-hugging denim
posturing under a mirror ball like
the purple Prince himself.

Nothing between us, just laughter and glitter,
but love was a prick you said: tomorrow
you will find me a grave man.

I thought you would be here forever;
at first you stayed so alive.

You asked at the crematorium if we could
arrange for sparklers in your casket.

In the cinder-block hospital room
windowless fake-light fluorescence

machines whirring behind bed curtains billowing
reluctant wings. You woke to say it was raining

outside. I walked into a summer downpour
knowing you were flying: mercurial and fantastic
and I cried.

Bargaining with Water
for Alan Kurdi and the many nameless children of the sea

Voice of ancient water, wine-dark Sea of Ulysses,
the one who knows no borders, conjoiner of the deeps –
She opened her mouth and said: Come!

Sea with the voice of all exiles cried out:
I will cool the fires that burn your homes.
Leave behind the flames of ISIS and Assad.
Bring your loved ones to me. I will wash them of the soot
of war. I will take the sound of explosions from their ears.
I am the salt tears of drowned sailors.

Rehanna replied,
I am terrified of water. I have carried my children
over so many borders, through the dust and smog
of crowded cities, through camps without food
or sewers. I meet with dusk at azure's edge
with motherland soil packed under my nails.
My children know the ancestral desert
that lives in the dust of my hair.

Voice of the Sea said,
I will wash you clean. I will offer you rest. I will silence
the drone strikes. I will make visible those the world refuses
to see. Give me your children. I will give you pearls for eyes.
I am the Sea of never-forgetting. I will tell your story.

Rehanna spilled from the broken raft, her children
slipping through father's fingers, into waves of eternity,
following thousands who silently perished.

The Sea took her youngest child, folded him in her arms
washing him gently orphaned on the shore: clean
beautified, beatified, no longer the son of Rehanna
but the child of headlines world-wide.

And the Sea rejoiced,
I am the hope of displaced millions. More will come.
For all those who know this road from Damascus
may scales now fall from your eyes.

Atom-Bomb Nostalgia

I. The Canadian Shield

Raised in the Cold War, surviving on the Rock
of Joni Mitchell and The Guess Who. We grew
storied here with atom-bomb nostalgia. Now we
glow iridescent as our half-life declines.

I thought I knew your landscape, your deep lake,
and greener ache for untamed space.

This was our strange arcana: ICBMs, KGB,
peace on vinyl, LSD. We spoke like English
queens by grade thirteen, French kissing,
lusting girl-tongued with lavender prose.
We bloomed as wallflower children,
decommissioning nuclear families.

Encoding our lips with tribade vows,
fingers entwined in bowers
of downstream dark forests.
You were my fallout shelter.

Half our lives we loved
as large as this vastness:
A mari usque ad mare.

I mapped our legacies' displaced parents
whose wars had redrawn borders
whose accents made them as foreign
then as we are to each other now.

II. Niagara Falls

Its flow erodes bedrock. The scene abuzz.
Scavenger gulls taking flight in the widening
gorge. Me, overeating steam-pan scrambled
eggs and pale pancakes. You, overlooking
ice-encased cascades, the fun-house arcades
and wax museum likenesses. *Believe It or Not*
love ends here: an uneasy Easter Sunday
and lineups at the casino.

I have never gambled with slot machines or cards.
I have never diced away hope or your robes for gold.
I have never believed that a boulder could roll from a
tomb, but you could move the rock that sealed this cave
with merely your lips on my thigh –
high-wire tightrope delights; a Great Wallenda
wagering us against the final plunge.

III: Cataracts

Falling water, failing vision.
You know I can see the border from here.

Monsters in the mist make shapes. You see strange
angels; their protean wings soar into outrage.

I skate softly on the eggshells
of your time-bomb mind.

IV. Magnetic North

Lost attractions. I tried drawing you back, searching
sunless arctic skies for full moons, for skyrocket
desire, sentimental space-junk memories in meaningless
orbit, uncoupled cake pans, indivisible duvets, queen
sheets, pillows and pillow shams;

paths turned riddles, rooted as trees. Noisy clouds recalling
your breath but not your words. We could have claimed
early pensions: settled in amiable discontent for
colonial rocking-chair futures.

Maybe you romance the good old days of nuclear
proliferation to our record-player protest songs.
Don't you wish we were young again,
waiting for the world to end?

V: Perennial Borders

Root-bound beds of false indigo and bleeding
hearts gate the empty house. Displaced, I am
foreign as before.

I alone face the soothsayer at Departures
at the sign for checking extra baggage.

She riffs me into this new urban beat
till I sing, "I must let go of you now;
I must let go to be free."

Runway lights, feeling the lift
and brightening air: a new sun floating
shadows of wings on the clouds below.

Another Poem about a Rose

A rose by any other name
would smell

the same as these faded dry
flowers smell
saved from a love
long left now.

They smell like dry sonnets
in musty books,
outdated conceits,
rose-dust that clings
to a maudlin mind.

A moldy rose smells rank, like
an old sandwich made with tender
thoughts but forgotten in the fridge
behind condiments rarely used:

old mustard, gherkins,
that anonymous sauce I think
you used to like but I cannot
throw away despite its
un-relishing smell.

A rose is a rose is a rose, said
Gertrude Stein: her line
dulling long dead tropes;
dead before these thorns grew
or this blossom dried.

I almost refuse to purge, until a tiny
angry spider emerges, disturbed
from this dead
finely-webbed floral shell:
alive in her venomous home
where our love used to dwell.

A Lonesome Lesbian Doughnut Encomium

Autumn, fresh and Maple-Frosted, came calling.
Rising romance wafted through tall shelves.
I met you in the café near the open stacks.

You parted your lips for a Double-Chocolate Dip
and spoke with freshly minted phrases,
kissing our newly wise words into warm couplets.

The sweet hungry dawn arrived before we could sleep,
baking our naked bodies caffeine-thin.

You reminded me of summer:
fresh strawberry nipples decorating your creamy breasts,
sweetly filling Old-Fashioned Plain afternoons.

Where high art rose, I fell for you,
Honey Dipped, sticky and sweet,
a snatch all natural and sugar free.

But dull winter set in and we bickered, bitter and cold.
I eat and eat, sugar-stupid and starved for
Vanilla Filled nights, our love-crumbs stale now.

I go lonely to the café, order my coffee
Double-Double: like spells of Shakespearian witches,
brewed beyond brown. I ask for the baked goods
that embody us now: one Frosted
Cruller and a muffin. I devour you in effigy,

my eyes hazing over in the Glazed Sour Cream.

My hips have grown to fill the space
where your hips once pressed,
yet I am an empty centre.

Parting Ways
for Jaqueline Faeredelune Fassel

Jacquie came back
on Christmas Day as
a trove of white ashes,
a compound of bone dust and
Viking dress in winter's limbo.

When spring arrived, you
and your little boy
met with her coven
on a greening hill near
her favourite tree.

You waved hello
to her cousins,
as if you saw them
walking up the path –
yet they were stuck
for hours on a stalled train.

You must have seen their *fetch*
said her friends.
The veil is thin today.

When all were gathered
together you spooned her:
white powder into
deep brown live earth, and
everyone parted ways.

My Dead Poet

imagines shoveling rocky syllables
hand stained with hard-word callouses
of playwright, shipwright, plough-wright,
shoulder to the wheel

emulating dying hands, colourful artisans,
hammers at a forge: wise shades whose
earthling worms shimmer gooey
on skull-bone bits.

Oh Whitman! My late captain,
are you more relevant than the living?
Explain us now to ourselves! I wonder what
I shall impart with my bones calcifying dirt.

Shall I study now in charnel houses?
Suture together a monstrous outsider
electrified against night skies?
Be intertextual like a zombie,
fed on others' brains?

I require bright plumes of ink and all my muses:
chorus lines of glamourous trans-kin,
motorbike wymyn in cool black leather,
V-twin engines humming between their legs,

and one nubile coiffeur who is oh so steamy:
clit-cloven jeans, hairdryer and iron so hot
she could have been a blacksmith.

I stare too long at her dyer's hand
and her beauty-school chewing gum lips,
no lingering stench of renaissance men.

I am lost to careless lovers' old disease:
the lusting physiologies of stories lodged
with beetles in my broken mouth.

I want fresh composition, beauty, form,
poetic feet, metrical hair. I am grateful for
this body, this animation of my soul:
freckled skin, scars, cellulite, and longing.

O smithy's forge, O dyer's hand, invent me.

Letting Go

She has let herself go,
has left sleep in her eyes
and dreams in her hair.

She has let herself go to seed,
let the tractor rust in the field
and the laundry out flapping on the line.

She has let her plumpness
breathe un-girdled; walks barefoot
in rain through the unmown lawn.

She has abandoned widow's weeds
and wedding band; thought less
about his granite headstone,
his clock-maker's precision.

She still has a number
pinned to the wall
on yellowing paper
over a black
rotary phone.

She will call –
she will say she loves
this daughter who
let herself go   free.

Empty Urn

You were the sky-gazer, brooder of storm clouds,
mind nesting in oviform threats: zeppelins,
cluster bombs, wingless grenades. We were
thawing from so many Cold War lies.
I thought you had joined me in peace.

Hawk-eyed, you spied Bolsheviks
in boxes under the bed, in sepia photos
a boy who would have been your great uncle
had he not been caught in the crossfire of the
October revolution

years before Stalin scorched your grandmother's
Baltic farm. Soviet soldiers torturing chickens,
children, old folk-dancing servants: raping women
who dared to speak your mother's mother tongue.

You always knew, you said,
someone would push the button
blowing us to Hiroshima:

freeze-frame shadows,
funereal ashes, perfect figures
on Keats's Grecian Urn.

You, riven, embodied ink-veined letters,
DP camp mementos, old monochrome film
rolls developed as family-tree pogroms and purges.
You gnawed long nights on soup-bones of the
deceased, waking to alarm-clock legends
with scrambled morning's shell-shocked

eggs. Your mother, a child, hid in the henhouse:
Red Army driving nails into the eyes of farm boys.
She found a headless Russian soldier in her garden,
your grandmother stewing traumas into
all the generations of her borscht.

You curled fetal, fearful in fallout shelters,
digging deeper as your penumbra family chased
you in cracking sunlight into shadow factions –

your brother, then your sisters, out to get you;
our children hatched into spies and thieves as
Uncle Joe beat you with his Khrushchev shoe.

                    **

This war could only end when you
dropped the bomb.

I am the enemy.

The little possum who drowned
in our basement window-well that terrible
rainy summer told you so.

I am dead to you, and you to me, yet
no ashes fill an urn.

Somewhere you are feeding the cats, brushing your teeth.

Now I am free and far away. I dance with my
true love to *our silent music's perfect sounds.*

I scarcely recall you, except in passing troubled strangers
with fierce eyes, shaking with fear: palsied junkies, mad
shouting women: veterans of second-hand wars whose
names will not inscribe a flower-laden cenotaph.

Those brave undead, they howl:
"*Beauty is truth* means nothing:
        an empty phrase
        on an empty urn."

I would have passersby salute their noisy wounds,
drape them in flags, but I glimpse your shadow
waving and I wake from feathery-pillowed
sleep, shaking my fist at the bright
Enola Gay.

Love's Atlas

When the world is at peace, I will lift you to my strong
shoulders, run exultant along beauty's lush boulevards
into the mirthful houses of Baghdad and Damascus,
through Saharan fountains, sprouting verdant orchards,
grafted apples from the fertile unfenced gardens
        of Riyadh, and Cairo, and Gaza, and Tel Aviv.

When the world is at peace, I will carry you down
to the rivers of the Holy Land: the Limpopo,
the Congo, the Zambezi – every river, a primal mother
who washed our unbleached, unfaded, unscarred
        perfect nascent skin.

We will flow through the mild Nile, the protective
Tigris, and her mate, the Euphrates, the bare-breasted Amazon,
the orgasmic O's of the Oronoco, the sisterhood of the Missouri and
the Mississippi, where the strange misnomer of miscegenation
        exists as kisses of love on mixed lips.

As we drift north, I will guide you through colder waters,
bereft brides of colonial lords, their maiden names erased:
the Hudson, the St. Lawrence, the Mackenzie, the Red River –
all free waters, when they spoke their native
        clear blue names.

When the world is at peace, we will climb into thin ether
into sublime peaks of Everest and Kilimanjaro,
through old Alleghenies, ancient Appalachians
who were mountains long before
        such appellations.

When the world is at peace, we will walk hand in hand
like when we were each other's better selves, before hatred,
shrapnel, and empty shelves. When Atlas shifted the world,
you dropped me, and I dropped you, we became
        the fallen.

When we were young, I wondered how others
confused or benumbed or ungrateful in life
would sully this sacred world with loveless
        spineless, useless strife.

Curating the Anthropocene

In collective notations from the outer rims
of our ending selves, we'll observe our fossil
record eroding in acid oceans,
the last of our effluent feeding some
noxious algae, now extinct.

We will become sentimental,
longing for who we were.

Our after-selves will make
big budget musicals,
dramatizing the glamour of
vast transgenic wheat fields,
gleaming satellites crowding night skies.

Ushers providing the softest tissues
for our liquifying eyes, just before the
house lights go up and we hear
the last blast of applause.

When the end arrives, we will teach our children
to wave goodbye to the closing sunset,
misty-eyed for all our grandeur of invention.

We will leave legacy landfill for future
post-humans naturally curious about
our cast-offs.

They will regale us, unique among species
for self-reflection, iconic statues, self-abasing art –
poetic venerations of our angst.

Beyond our own disposability,
a voice in the next epoch fledges
a new kind of bird
we never live to see.

She calls out to the
greatness of nothing
a song that invents her only
for one moment at a time.

Part II: Blood Moon

Divining

Back to the depths
site of evolution
our bodies pooling

droplets, forming waves
grinding rock into sand.

Salt water forms puddles on sheets,
deepens, sets us adrift, flooding into
thundering rivers, cresting,

the becoming of sinew strain and lung breath.
Our tributaries engineer streams of limbs,
flesh between breasts and knees.

If words could force the taste of wet on my teeth,
the ocean of this bed, your navel a sea

dripping hot from unbraided mane to untamed belly,
your forest of hair, this Venus shore, trembling fingers
entwined. Diving down. Swimming.

If words could summon the body of you here,
invisible pores beading wet above your lips, or

if I could be called to where you are: Istanbul, Cappadocia,
Sarasota, the North Saskatchewan River, a port on
the Sea of Japan, then be

a spell: coral lips, pierced earlobes, fluttering lashes,
soft but muscled arms.

Water-witch: I divine you in subterranean rivers
in deep thoughts:

you of blue veined skin; a pulse
differentiating life from tidal rhythm,

or if you cannot be conjured here,
be the smell of a gathering storm on the wind.

Apocalypse: A Love Song

The apocalypse came: I lost my wife,
the house, three adored cats, a green backyard,
a jar of delicate seashells, two treasured china cabinets,
linen towels, a Linden tree sheltering a birdbath,
lilacs, and the perennial bee balm.

I walked for the last time on the East Shore beach
bidding goodbye to the doomsday nuclear reactor
silhouetted against the irrecoverable skyline. Invasive
super-sized occasional corpses of day-glow orange carp
lay on the shore.

After the apocalypse, the world lay
warhead-scorched and tsunami sunk.
I thought of all the things I should have done.
I should have read the signs. I should have seen it coming.
I should have repented before it was too late.
I should have filed my taxes on time, flossed more
often, spent more time with the kids. I should have
put away my laundry before it wrinkled, my face too –
I should have stayed young longer, slept on a slant board
to keep my breasts from sagging. I should
have fought gravity, fought for my rights, been
less obstinate, more compliant, kept the kitchen clean,
lost twenty pounds, spent less, saved more, not squandered
my time on financial crises, wasting waking hours riding
the angst-ridden bête-noir horses of what might befall.

After the apocalypse, I began to hear strange noises, odd voices –
a ridiculous inner adolescent self, flirting with first love, foolishly
filling verses with sliver-lining cloud clichés, and those hackneyed
cracks in the sidewalk where straggling rainbow blossoms push
through crumpled cement, sprouting new green growth. . .

You, smiling, joyously giddy here, a ball of clay rolling
between the tip of your thumb and forefinger, an increasing
orb, rolling rounder in your perfect palms.
You, filling up oceans, moulding mountains, laughing in
post-apocalyptic cold with me at the midnight empty streetcar stop,
reveling in our newness, pitying history's bickering blights of
dead world dramas, those tiny, tragic landscapes receding
with grace, as you dance the new Earth alive.

Mending Descartes

I am. Thinking
I am. You are:
Impoverished soul.
Divider of self.
Denier of body.
Of Matter.
Of Materiality:
Dog Pain.
Cat Souls.

I am
Hands
Typing
I am a
Hand that joins

I am. Finding my own
Mind. Body. Animal.

I am   thinking –
hands   typing
body   finding
connecting/breathing

I did not intend to be a seamstress
to say it is women's work
to stitch old men back together
or heal the cults of long division
the graphing of selves on
Cartesian planes

I am only moving my material
mouth – tongue against teeth
against those who deny I am
as real as dog dreams –
twitching paws. You see
my tracks typed here

I am body-imbedded thought,
neurotransmitters, muscle memory,
animal pleasures, hands joining,
warming others' hands –
un-split, I am.

Blood Moon

Full, carrying low:
pain is labour's synonym.
Why have you not taught

painters to draw dark
eyes on tired Madonnas
when sleeplessness is

truth? Why do you fill
asylums? Mothers tortured
by Hallmark myth cards.

Make old Pietàs
display reshaped Marias
with muscular arms.

Reveal white-haired crones,
beautiful, wise survivors
of lies that nearly

broke them. Tell your cults
of virgins to beware of
angels in chains. They

are false idols. Speak
full truths, for your devotees
will be astronauts.

Mrs. John H. Nicely

My Aunt Helen, spry at 93 –
her 20/20 vision sees everything
there is, and often more.

Stays enlivened by imagined slights,
the constant excitement of terrible news,
televangelists, and several loving cats.

Survivor of the Great Depression,
childhood beatings, a madwoman,
mother, and working for a living
while men went off to war.

She used to buy me western
boots and cap guns and
cowgirl dresses with holsters.
She called me Little Princess.

Markswoman, NRA-dead eye,
revolver under her pillow,
a believer in female silence –
and power.

She has managed every funeral
for over 70 years.

She believes in womanly virtues:
good hygiene and obscurity;

despises promiscuous self-revelation
and crypto-Catholic confessions
disguised as poetry, sees celebrity
as Papal opulence diluted.

"There is only one eternal book," she says,
and prays to find her name
imprinted there as "Mrs.
John H. Nicely."

How strange and cruel would it be
if she found herself honoured here?

Family of Five Sonnets:

i: My Father

I am a writer of guilt lists, should-haves;
I am the writer who never writes
to others, who lies awake at night
regretting unwritten letters

to people dead now or moved
to other lives and lost to me. If I
could write to you, my father,
I would say,

when you died I finally opened, free
of judgment, not because I lost my fear of
absolutism, or sarcasm, or the long
guns behind bedroom doors, but

I saw your fragility in an open casket. Then
I could have found you gentle if you came alive.

ii: Great Aunt Gladys

I never knew we were the poor cousins.
Hand-me-downs arrived from mythic relations:
fat boy trousers from Elwood in Ohio,
polyester pantsuits from a libber in New York.

I ripped the seams, recut lines along vogue tissue
patterns held with found pins. I sometimes
reimagined styles without templates –
re-stitched, re-embodied, made anew.

I still fashion myself in others' discards:
thrift-stores of random images, mixed debris,
rag-bag strips of wedding tulle, salvaged buttons.
I once patched my jeans with bits of a real silk scarf

from Great Aunt Gladys, who had a baby out of wedlock
in the 30s with a Jewish carnie she met on her flying trapeze.

iii: Sonnet as Retreat

Intimacy: a tiny-house loft bed,
rhymed quatrains, chants in a witch's
empty cottage, or a Grace Street
narrow row-house, opulent with

front yard bean stocks, marble tile &
Madonna niche on 13 feet of frontage.
We crave Lilliputian luxuries, posh stones
sparkling under the jeweler's intricate lens.

The first time a sonnet compared a lover's
mouth to roses it surprised us, descant
floating high above iambic downbeats;
pocket where the sacred and demonic came to love.

Together alone: microcosm begemmed by your red-rose lips
and a window. One small curtain covers all the world.

iv: Sonnet of Daybreak

You author
        the morning – making coffee,
        patiently waking the story
        of every day.

I dream of fleeing
        explosions, flights of insects,
        hurricanes, winged lions
        fast as meteors in the dark.

I cover my head with the last part of sleep,
        pull down skies full of thunderbirds
        (shining jets) wrapping around myself
        the chaos of blankets, fighting off

morning, fearing the leash of day. The sun wakes also
on this tether. You have let it out to graze.

v: Singularity

I could travel fast forever – vintage Mustang
convertible, low against the blacktop
coarse grit on the rumble-strip
hugging tarmac, aiming for take-off,

our faces hair-slapped by the wind.
I want to be the sun. I want to be forever.
I want to be deep, cloudless, bright, singular.
I am tempted to cut off lines with end rhymes,

nervous about white space, enjambed, anxious,
fearing paralysis at bus stops, panicked by inertia.
You tell me to be grateful for stalled trains, long
queues, for arriving early and waiting in the cold,

slackening lines, opening the waiting space, being
small in the infinite dome of winter's crepuscular sky.

Summer Canning

Widdershins clock, spell
pagan magic. Make the word
'tongue' taste. Make us pant

artifacts into being:
paint bombs of graffiti love,
or loaded brushes

dripping on canvas:
bright nudes with live lips that part
with our love, no more.

We could put down this
lavish joy crop for winter
when fresh bliss runs thin,

sterilizing joy;
a full, rolling boil keeps
jars from exploding

on pantry shelves. These
summer yellow words, preserved
like bright half peaches.

Toward a Lunch Break in Bed on a February Afternoon

I dash to you in the noonday rush, but subway's down;
the shuttle bus, a persistent crush
of elbow points, the ragged cold:
my quest for the edge of the world is sharp.
The lower jaws of jagged mountains bite the skin of the sky.

I trawl with throngs as the hooks and skeins
of the city hide beneath the wash of human tide.
My quest for the edge of the world is blunt.
The hammering seas strike like a clock on the
final shore, a battered dock at the firmament's end.

I gallop apace to the edge of the world,
urging on the fiery steeds, a Phoebus ride.
I meet you in horizonless skies
where the world has lost its edge.

In the slipping tide, we die and die: a plunging rush
in the sea of your eyes. We are pearl divers skimming
the afternoon sun from our shimmering, pulsing, aging skin.

I conjure a beach-house here for you by the Great Abyss.
Waves pass us through.
Our shuddering monsters sing

and we cry to the cuntless mermaids
who gather to envy our mortal grasping
at time.

Still Waters Run

Still waters do not run deep.
Still waters do not run.
Still waters stand
in stagnant ponds
breeding soft-minded
amoebas and mosquitoes.
Troubled waters stand still: diseased
brooding – disconsolate, self-absorbed – if the self
could absorb itself and still be (still) water.

Deep waters roll
in the engines of Leviathan's
grumbling stomach, in the will
to catch prey, to stay alive,
to eat another someone
who always tries to run terrorized
to save itself. This is Intelligent Design
defined: that we are mere sustenance to
the hungrier. Even mouthless
carrots scream and cling to earth.

High water mark – the apex, a personal best:
the plot point where the hedge fund collapsed,
the hurricane receded, where we
thought we had saved each other from
drowning, but found we were naturally buoyant.

Ancient whales bellyache,
resist all cults of being saved.
They cough up indigestible patriarchs, indifferent
to the plights of Job, Jonah, Captain Ahab,
spitting the bitter aftertaste of old-type
prefiguring. For Jesus was a whaler
leaving footprints on the water, a fisher of
us mammals on Golgotha's ivory shore.

Still waters do not run. They crawl
with decay. Waterlogged zealots (our former oppressors)
spawn malarial sporozoans, cholera, nostalgia, epidemics of
shame sermons, shallow and stagnant. They fish and fish
at Nineveh's shore for us on bent hooks, in rusted prayer.
But we aren't there. We dive to find what lies beneath,
where hungry whales of keener minds run deep.

In the Mind of My Familiar

I am cat queen of
creature comforts, fur coated,
wrapped against winter.

Slow riser, nesting
in down duvets. Eyes squint at
sunlight-drenched windows.

Rubbing against your
thigh: alarm clock agnostic
and pleasure desperate.

Indiscriminate
rosy-tongued in blood-rare beef.
My old animal

purrs primordial –
capturing the tender heart
of a slow gazelle.

Part III: Eurycleia

Eurycleia

Eurycleia has no English –
points to racks of coloured
polish for the feet she
washes. Sweeps the
clippings, nails and skin.

Men as well come here for
treatments. They of mid-
life girth and torpor:
former heroes, roaming
quest-less, but for wordless
happy endings.

Eurycleia
mapping bodies
owns their stories,
has a language.

She can read your every
secret scar.

Ekphrasis on Icarus, Winter Solstice Eve

I.
Let us raise a glass
to the once-strong sun
the now dying sun to

master builders
and master painters
master debaters
brilliant masters
inventors of Swiss watches
and assembly lines
inventors of leisure time

time to walk on the moon
to play at space-war ballistics.

Joyful we first were in ourselves:
clean, clothed, unexposed, raising
this delicate glass to a gold-digging
master. He strip-mined his Ganymede boys,
stripping gild from drag queens and
grace from lap-dancing mothers,
stripping powerful wings from
indigenous girls who vanished: the
expendable, unreported, unseen. He,
above reproach, golden, rose

to rule the sun almost
before his waxen wings began
to melt and he like Icarus

scorched by his dying sun
fell past golden bank towers
past barge and carrack
plunging through a sea
slick with oil
on canvas

past a simple ploughman
who simply looked
the other way.

II.
I confess my love for
indoor plumbing
cloud-hooded towers
cell phone apps
pharmaceutical antidepressants
and protection from the cold.

I could stare forever at the
limbo photo of Falling Man
and the art of old worlds lapsing
from Ovid to Brueghel.

No one saw the plunge
the white legs in water
except your sister: psychic
hotline dominatrix, slow
sky gazer, seer of polyamorous
park-sex queers, menopausal
insomniacs, one-eyed veterans
and feral children sleeping
with one eye open
all the time waiting
for their own delicate
splash into greatness,
eternal ripples stretched
in gilded frames on gallery walls.

I confess I have earned my master's
degree and PhD.

I have pried at locks secured
by old men lecherous with wisdom.
I have begged to propagate their lore.

Yet I will never be a Fellow
of the College.

I have seen old deans,
politicians preening feathers
plucked from others' wings.
We eager fledglings hit alluring
glass ceilings even as we watched

an aging academic sing
his auto-defenestration blues
riding his last bottle of single-malt scotch
into a clear dispassionate sky,
as the window closed behind him.

Shunned and sometimes unhygienic
I have a deep secret love for old books,
shelves of dynasties tumbling –
the yellowed verses of Wystan
Auden, creeper of schoolboys.

Smell the unfiltered stench of his
nicotine teeth. See how he shuffles in dirty
bedroom slippers through a cold Belgian
gallery of drowsy Dutch Masters.
painting on painting. He tucks
a pencil behind his ear until

hearing, like no one else, a delicate splash –
Icarus falling from Brueghel's
Renaissance sky where everyone,
even then –

or at some other time – that particular past
you always say is better than now –

even then we were all too busy
to notice; to hear the trotting of a
soft hoof, or troops of foot and horse,
or thundering Luftwaffe rising
to Wagner; falling to my father's
Howitzer blast in enemy
Messerschmitt fragments.

I have heard the sharp report
of a victory model revolver trigger
locked in his shell-shocked hands, in his
faulty love, in constant fear of the tyrant
powers he grasped at and revered.

III.
When I was nine, I saw a man
plunge from the sky: Trenton Airshow
Snowbird formation acrobatics
pilot upside down in his glass
bubble cockpit, his clear silhouette
low overhead; engines screaming.
He ejected too late; stillborn parachute,
fireball flash, snowing exploded wings in
light slivery pieces falling down upon us.
A crowd hungry for souvenir manna
fought over pieces
of his broken plane.

Just last spring, a flight of 300
vanished off radar leaving no mark
on the sea.

The second that summer, downed
over Ukraine: earth-strewn corpses
broken and looted: Malaysian suns
erupting again on its wings.

What hubris declared the newsman
to fly so close to hot-zones.

We heard the Russian
troops and we echoed that
kicking of Brown Shirt Nazi boots:
the ones in our front closet
the ones we always all have
worn in our relentless
fascist time machines:
the cotton gin
the slave-ship
the slave-whip
the micro-chip.

Please turn off your cell phones.
Hold down the button at the top until
the screen goes black and you can't
see what time it is, and you have to
hear the terrifying sound of your breath
going in and out and in and the people
beside you who are also making that
terrifying sound.

Under the shadow
of a master's gaze
under the drone
under the bomb-hatch
Aleppo is falling
Mozul is burning
Damascus is bleeding.
We are watching.

Now look at this small thing
in the dust, this little hoof
print, so you can see
where the torturer's horse [still, casually]
scratches its innocent behind on a tree:
an image so exact I had to smuggle it
in for you.

When I try to imagine a faultless love
or the life to come, writes Auden,
what I hear is the murmur of underground
streams, and what I see is a limestone landscape.

In reading these lines
I hear that murmur of
voices under limestone
under ice under water frozen above:
snowflakes falling like broken wings
have fallen softly and some have landed
safely on this silent night, have landed on
candlelit eulogies sung in this crisp winter air
in this moment of faultless love.

On this singular solstice eve, I feel
the cold-heartedness of the whole world
condensing onto one small ornate pane
of window frost with a smaller transparent dot.
This is the mark where the impress of
my now-warm fingerprint has melted
a tiny spyhole, an impermanent record of
my own DNA on these cosmic white swirls
of winter glass.

Apotheosis

You
brush back your hair
sip from a glass
not because your
hair troubles your face
or you thirst for a drink
but because these are
the gestures that
Beautify the World.

Acknowledgements

I am very grateful to Quattro Books, and to Kate Marshall Flaherty, for this wonderful opportunity. Huge thanks to Dane Swan, my keen and intuitive editor, and to thoughtful close readers Stanley Fefferman, Roz Spafford, and Tamara Cosby.

"Letting Go" appeared in *Temenos: Hidden in Sight* (Fall 2017). www.temenosjournal.com.

"Love's Atlas" appeared in *Dovetails: An International Journal of the Arts,* 2016.

Quattro's Best New Poets in Canada 2018

Tara Borin

Tara Borin's work has appeared online and in print in journals throughout Canada and the US, and in the anthology *Resistance*, edited by Sue Goyette (Coteau Books). Originally from London, Ontario, she now lives and writes in Dawson City, Yukon, in traditional Tr'ondëk Hwëch'in territory. She can be found online at taraborinwrites.com.

Sarah Kabamba

We are surrounded by stories and poetry. Sarah Kabamba just wants to share some of them with you. She was the winner of *Room Magazine*'s 2017 Emerging Writer Award and was shortlisted for the 2017 CBC Poetry Prize. Her work has been published in *Room Magazine, The New Quarterly, HA&L Magazine, Canthius,* and *In/Words Magazine and Press*. She is of Congolese origins, and now lives in Ottawa.

Georgia Wilder

For the past four years, Georgia Wilder has hosted Wild Writers, a monthly poetry salon in Toronto's Kensington Market. During this time, her writing has been nominated for The Journey Prize, The Humber Literature Review Contest, and the Peter Hinchcliffe Award. Her stories and poetry have appeared in several literary journals. An earlier play *Patricides* won Best Production in the Hart House Drama Festival. She teaches academic writing at the University of Toronto.

Other Recent Quattro Poetry Books

Brace Yourselves by Rocco de Giacomo
A tattered coat upon a stick by Christopher Levenson
Odysseus by Carl Hare
Home Was Elsewhere by Stanley Fefferman
Perfect Day by Leif E. Vaage
Barbaric Cultural Practice by Penn Kemp
Hyaena Season by Richard Osler
Poet, Painter, Mountain: After Cezanne by Susan McCaslin
The Resumption of Play by Gary Geddes
Love Learned by Barry Olshen
Hermit Thrush by Mark Frutkin
Running on the March Wind by Lenore Keeshig
Midnight by Ian Burgham
Georgia and Alfred by Keith Garebian
Stone Soup by Kate Marshall Flaherty
The Hundred Lives by Russell Thornton
Night Vision by Christopher Levenson
Pin Pricks by Phlip Arima
Under the Mulberry Tree edited by James Deahl
Come Cold River by Karen Connelly
Beyond Mudtown by Rob Rolfe
And the cat says… by Susan L. Helwig
Against the Flight of Spring by Allan Briesmaster
The Rules of the Game by Ludwig Zeller
Too Much Love by Gianna Patriarca
parterre by elías carlo
Night-Eater by Patricia Young
Fermata by Dennison Smith
Little Empires by Robert Colman
nunami by Barbara Landry
One False Move by Tim Conley
Where the Terror Lies by Chantel Lavoie
Something Small To Carry Home by Isa Milman
jumping in the asylum by Patrick Friesen
Without Blue by Chris D'Iorio
When the Earth by Lisa Young
And tell tulip the summer by Allan Graubard
Book of Disorders by Luciano Iacobelli